Run a Marathon like You Run a Business!

(or the other way around)

I0390415

Gunnar Thorsén

www.runners42195.com

DEDICATION

To Hugo, Erik, Sofía Thorsén

CONTENTS

PREFACE

The name of this book, Runners42195, is inspired by the distance, 42.195 meters (46,145 yard), of a marathon. I strongly believe that any healthy person is capable of running a marathon if they have the right motivation, physical training and mental skill sets. The marathon represents a tough challenge, both physically as well as psychologically, but with all of these factors in place the chance of success is very high.

The content and message of this humble piece of "literature" is applicable to anyone with similar ambitions and conditions regardless of your nationality and current whereabouts whether it is Chicago, Shanghai, Madrid, Stockholm or elsewhere.

CHAPTER 1
THE CONCEPT

I have found and been able to confirm several parallels between running a business and the experience of preparing, running and finishing successfully the full 42.195 meters (46,145 yard) of a marathon. By identifying the underlying values that are the foundations and key to success with a marathon, we can directly apply this to our daily reality as business professionals. Interestingly enough, the opposite is perfectly possible as well, applying business strategies to prepare and run a marathon.

This book will help you to develop the skill set necessary for successfully preparing and running a marathon and use it directly as a business professional to better run your Business.

For more inspiration and continuous updates visit www.runners42195.com

Let me share with you some examples of what I see as shared values between running a marathon and running a business.

Gunnar Thorsén

CHAPTER 2
ATTITUDE

"If you think you can, or you think you can't, you're right!"

Although this is the first section of the first chapter The Concept, it is actually the last contribution to the book. This chapter captures the essence of the book as everything at the end is about attitude. You may lack or skip one of the other topics in this book and still make it to the finish line at the marathon or still launch and maintain a business, but without the right attitude you will have no chance of success. Of course attitude alone is not enough, but here is where it all starts.

I gave this topic a lot of thought and this is my firm conviction;

Anyone that wants to run a marathon can do so. Anyone that wants to run a business can do so.

End of story.

Of course not everyone can be as good as Bekele in the marathon or as successful as Steve Jobs in business, but that is a different topic.

Gunnar Thorsén

CHAPTER 3
AMBITION

"Ambition is putting a ladder against the sky."

Just the fact that you have decided to run a marathon is a sign of ambition as it is a challenge for most people that will require time, determination, sacrifice and effort. On top of that it is voluntary and you normally end up paying money to do it!

In a marathon preparation there are three basic goals:

1-show up on race day

    2-finish the race

        3-reach your race objective

Ambition is about **pushing your limits** and reaching goals that are at the very limit of your capacity.

I have full respect for anyone who sets their marathon objective to "enjoy the race". However this book is about setting and reaching specific objectives in a methodical way so we will go beyond this basic objective.

The objective, or goal, needs to be smart, S-M-A-R-T.

This is extremely important in any context whether it be running a marathon or running a business as objectives that don´t comply with this would be useless, counterproductive and demotivating.

Specific

  Measurable

    Achievable

      Relevant

        Time-bound

Let´s break down the S.M.A.R.T. concept considering preparing and running a marathon.

Specific - First you need to answer the five W´s:

Why? What? Who? When? Where?

Why do you run the marathon in the first place? From a personal experience this can be anything from having fun with friends to reaching an ambitious goal by pushing your limits.

What do you want to achieve? This can be reaching a specific race time, maintaining a regular contact with friends or it can be losing those extra 5 kg from last Christmas.

Who is of course YOU but also with whom together you plan to reach this goal.

When is the date of The Race.

Where is the place of The Race.

All of these W´s must be answered; it´s very important for the rest of the preparation and execution as it represent the Vision and project charter of your endeavor.

Measurable - The first two basic goals are easy to measure and so is the third, for example a race time under 3 hours and 30 minutes, or be among the 100 fastest in my category (this is measurable but you will not be able to monitor your performance during the race), improve my previous personal record by 10 minutes, etc. Avoid ambiguous or goals hard to define such as merely "enjoy running, improve physical strength or lose weight".

Achievable - As you will be setting your own goal for the marathon you need to be self-critic when doing so but do assure you ask for advice and the opinion of others before deciding on the final objective. Be realistic but also make sure you push your limits.

Relevant - This is the part of the soul-searching you need to do yourself. What is a relevant goal to you? It makes no sense to set an ambitious race time objective if reaching this goal makes no difference to you nor motivates you. The goal must feel important to you, important enough to guide and motivate you throughout the endeavor.

Time-bound - Link your objective and goal to an event, such as a specific marathon race and pin-point this event in your calendar. So whatever your goal is, aim to reach it at this event. This will implicitly lead to the need for organization as discussed in a later chapter in this book.

Example: I want to improve my last marathon time with 20 min and run sub 3 hours and 30 minutes. As a bonus objective I added to have fun training and running with my friends from the small group of runners from ESADE Business School in Barcelona, Spain.

Why is your business only local when it can be nationwide? Why is your business only nationwide when it can be global?

A business can be a way to pay the monthly bills, it can be a way of life, it can to out-beat competition, it can be to make competition irrelevant by creating a blue ocean or it can be something that changes people and even the world. The ambition level set by the founders or leaders of the company sets the direction for all activities and it will either motivate or demotivate the team. So pay close attention to the ambition level as it will be the spirit and guideline of the business.

Think big!

Kitchen blackboard with marathon race objective

Gunnar Thorsén

CHAPTER 4
COURAGE

"Courage is resistance to fear, mastery of fear, not absence of fear."

There is one certainty with preparing and running a marathon; there are uncertainties.

You may fail. You may get injured. You may not be able to follow your training schedule. You may not reach your race objective. Actually there is one more certainty; you will suffer. Still you pursue your objective knowing that in order to be a winner you must take the leap. You need courage and you need to be brave!

You may fail in business as well. We mostly hear of the great successes but reality shows that most start-ups fail.

Preparation and market intelligence will help you to take decisions but there will always be uncertainties in business as well. Some decisions are easier to take and some have limited impact on the overall results, others are tougher to take and some have severe impact on the bottom line. What they all have in common however is that they all have a certain degree of uncertainty and it takes courage to take business decisions, often implicating many other people both within and outside the company. It also takes courage to dare to be different in business, to pursue something not necessarily written in handbooks or covered by business school case studies.

Be brave!

Gunnar Thorsén

CHAPTER 5
ORGANIZATION

"In the beginning there was only Chaos."

Successfully preparing and running a marathon is not a coincidence, it requires planning with clear objectives, tasks and assigned resources.

First of all you need to establish your objective with preparing and running the marathon as the rest of the preparation will depend on the objective and your condition prior to this program. Establish your short, mid and long term S.M.A.R.T. business objectives and establish a detailed action plan with milestones and deadlines that you and your organization will stick to.

The organization of a marathon preparation can look like this:

Set your S.M.A.R.T. goal

See chapter Ambition for details on a good S.M.A.R.T. goal.

Pick the event

This will give you the frame work of the organization. How much time you have to prepare. Does it involve travelling to the race location, qualification requirements, special race location conditions such as altitude, temperature, terrain, etc.

Assess your resources available

Do you have previous marathon experience? If this is your first marathon you need to seek advice from experts and friends to prepare properly.

Are you regularly training already? You need a longer ramp-up period if you are not currently training regularly.

How many days and time each session can you train every week? Assure the training schedule is compatible with your other commitments, personal and professional.

Check the state of your running gear, especially the shoes. If you plan to acquire new shoes make sure you break them in well in advance of the race

Review your goal

Assure it remains S.M.A.R.T. If it does not, review and adjust all previous steps as long as necessary.

Prepare a detailed training plan

The detailed plan should include dates and times for training sessions (at least define if you will train early morning, during lunch or in the evening), distances, duration, intensity, training type (endurance, interval, fartlek, ascent, strength, etc.) all the way up to Race Day.

Example: To reach my objective I need to run 5 days per week (Monday, Tuesday, Thursday, Saturday and Sunday) during 20 weeks with the longer session on weekends. During weeks 8-16 I will run one interval session per week and progressively increase session duration during weekend runs up to a maximum two hour session.

Establish milestones throughout the training schedule and link them to sub-goals

These sub-goals will be your KPI´s so you can monitor the progress of your training and assure you stay on track to reach your main objective and goal. It is recommended to have at least one competition run, normally a half marathon about 1 to 1 ½ month prior the marathon race date. This is an important KPI and also a motivational factor as a part of the project.

My Saucony Zealots – discrete and very stealth

Execute your plan.

Don´t skip sessions, you cannot recover or compensate a session later since your training period is limited. Note: pay attention to what your body is telling you; perhaps your target was too ambitious.

Tired? You run!

Raining? You run!

Favorite show on TV? You run!

Barcelona-Madrid soccer game? You run!

Knees hurt badly? Now this is different. You need to pay attention to any signal from your body. If you have serious signs of injury you need to seek professional advice before you run again.

Race day

Set different objective levels.

This is a somewhat controversial statement. Some people might say it would be planning to fail. I don't agree. It´s true that if you think you will fail, for sure you will fail. However victory can come in different shapes and forms.

Your training plan should have been based on your most ambition objective to assure you actually aim for the stars. This objective must be S.M.A.R.T. On Race Day many external factors may affect you and having established alternative objectives and backup plans can assure that you still enjoy the experience.

In my 2012 marathon I achieved my personal best time ever improving the total time with over 20 minutes and these were my objectives:

Satisfied - sub 3h49m56s (my previous personal best)

Proud - sub 3h35m

YEAH! - sub 3h30m

During the race I always break down the race into accumulated objective split times for every five kilometers based on my most ambitious race time, YEAH! I then write them down on my hand on Race Day. I use these split times as my secondary KPI´s and monitor them during the race. As primary KPI I use the average time per kilometer and I try to stay 5-10 seconds below my target pace during the first half of the race and try to stay exactly on the target pace during the second part. This way I have a certain buffer when I reach The Moment of Truth as described in a later section in this book.

After the race

Be proud of your achievement and start planning for your next challenge, use the inertia and training you have built up to assure this becomes a sustainable change in your life.

Examples:

Run the same marathon next year with a more ambition objective.

Run another long-distance race in six months' time, again with my training buddies.

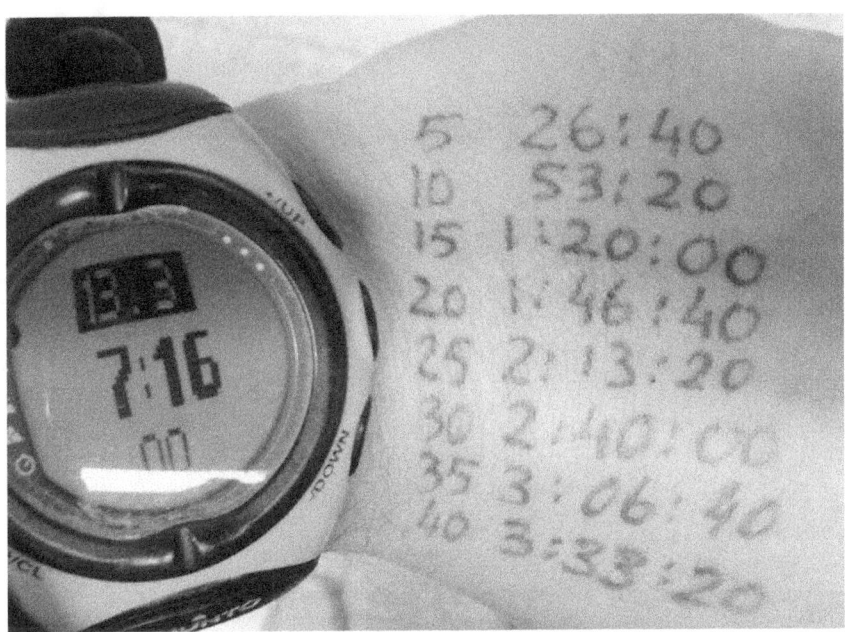

5k split times from my 2016 marathon with target time sub 3h 45m

Gunnar Thorsén

CHAPTER 6
TEAM SPIRIT

"As a team, we will heal"

Even if marathon running in itself is an individual activity the most successful runners will train and compete as part of a team. Get inspiration and advice from fellow runners and enjoy sharing your own experiences with others. Most of my running sessions are running alone but I have always shared my running and training experience with others in different ways. It can be talking with friends, writing blogs or joining an athlete club.

You can start a business on your own but you cannot turn it into a great success without the help from others. Create a strong Team, believe in your Team and inspire your Team.

When preparing a marathon you need to consider different areas such as aerobic training, strength training, running techniques, food and drinking habits, mental preparation etc. For a professional athlete different trainers and experts would support different parts of the training. For a non-professional you will do it yourself but surely you would look for input from different sources for all these areas. And the same goes for business.

You need different skill sets to set up and run a business so putting together a strong team is basically identifying the skills you need and find, recruit, retain and develop the talent within your team.

CHAPTER 7
DISCIPLINE

"Work hard, play hard"

Stick to the training schedule, also on that rainy Monday evening in January when you would rather stay at home watching a movie than putting on your running shoes and hitting the street for a 60 minute interval series session. In a dedicated training and preparation schedule missing one session will not ruin your chances of success, but missing several session certainly will. It is also important to understand that you cannot compensate later, or earlier, for a missed session. Adding intensity and or duration of a later session will not compensate the missed session and may even lead to injury.

Be disciplined and stay on schedule.

In business stay within areas where you can be number one or at least a close second, focus on your core business. Diversification may help you to minimize risk but if you stray into areas you don´t control, unless you enjoy a secure monopoly situation, you will run the serious risk of failure due to the simple fact that your competition is acting within their area of core competence. Don´t be tempted to deviate from your strategic plan and business model with every "unique" opportunity that comes up.

An upcoming thunderstorm that made me run 45 min in a skyfall.

January 11pm run with strong cold winds.

Gunnar Thorsén

CHAPTER 8
SACRIFICE

"No pain, no gain"

You will invest time and efforts to reach your objective. This will require sacrifice by you and your family not only on race day, but especially during the months of preparation.

To accumulate the weekly hours in your training schedule you will need to find time outside your work schedule and must-do family obligations so you will find yourself running at 6 am before breakfast, during the lunch break under the hot Madrid sun or just before midnight after dinner and putting the kids to bed. Most runners put their longer runs on weekends so this can easily take three to four hours from your weekend. Then of course there are the physical efforts of constantly increasing intensity and distance in your training assuring that you increase your capacity to match the objective you have established earlier.

Success in business comes from a little inspiration and a lot of hard work.

Whether or not you invest your own money in the business you will surely invest your time and energy to achieve your professional goals that will require sacrifice in other areas such as family and social life. Like when you missed the family BBQ at your best friend's house to get on that Sunday early morning flight with connection in Paris to make a 10 am Monday meeting in Shanghai. A ten hour flight in economy class with airline food, Adam Sandler movies, no sleep, no shower and no breakfast before you get into your meeting is enough to make a grown man cry.

CHAPTER 9
FLEXIBILITY

"A pessimist sees the difficulty in every opportunity; an optimist sees the opportunity in every difficulty."

Unforeseen events will always occur. A business trip you did not expect, illness, minor injury, family issues, etc. Prepare a backup plan. During the preparation of my 2012 marathon where I had set as my objective to reach a personal best time, I suddenly started to feel strong pain in my right knee during running practice. The pain was not too severe so I decided to not seek professional advice just yet. After a couple of running sessions the pain would not go away and was getting a little worse every session so I decided to make several changes to my preparation model in a last attempt to solve it myself. First I took one week off from running. This is a risky decision in a 14 week plan as you cannot recover or compensate for missed sessions. However my health was the highest priority so the decision was easy to make. Basically I made four simultaneous changes so obviously it was not a scientific approach in order to find the root cause to the problem but rather a pragmatic way to stay on track with my preparation in order to reach my objective.

The changes I made were: increased time for pre-run stretching, drinking a lot of water prior to running, buying new running shoes and finally I started taking Chondroitin and Glucosamine tablets with my meals. These substances are naturally found in our knees but with age and intensive training the lubrication of the joints may need some additional help. The result was that the pain gradually disappeared and after 2 weeks I had no more symptoms and have not had them since.

Even the best business plan is still only a plan based on projections. Make sure you can adapt to changing internal and external factors and still be true to your mission and vision. Make at least three projections; optimistic, realistic and pessimistic. Plan your business based on the realistic projection but assure you have plans for the optimistic and pessimistic scenarios that you can activate with short notice if required. Infrastructure and human resources are two areas to pay especial attention to as they are potentially slow to adapt to changing circumstances.

Berlin business trip in November – a 6am run to stay on schedule

Gunnar Thorsén

CHAPTER 10
PERSEVERANCE

"When the going gets tough, the tough gets going."

Follow through on your plan to reach your objective in accordance with your ambitions. Some may get offended by this statement but if you don´t reach your objective you have failed. Having said so failing is not necessarily bad, as long as you learn from it and improves as a person and as a professional. This book however is about how to reach your objective so let´s focus on one of the perhaps many times forgotten aspects of getting there, the ability to persevere.

Execute to perfection your established preparation schedule and complete the full 42.195 meters on race day.

Business success does not occur overnight, keep up the momentum throughout you planning horizon. Learn from the mistakes, don´t let it demotivate or stop you.

The Moment of Truth

This moment is part of the race and deserves a dedicated section of the book as it so crucial to the overall achievement of your objectives. If you are executing your race strategy in line with your race objective you will reach a point in the race, typically around the 30-35 km mark, when you feel that your body has run out of energy and your brain starts telling you to stop or slow down. This is commonly referred to as the Wall. I previously described the Key Performance Indicators I use during the race but during the final part of the race when I expect to reach my Moment of Truth I constantly monitor a third and less precise indicator, really more of a Key Risk Indicator (KRI); my relative speed. This is basically when a majority of fellow runners start to pass me as this indicates a slowdown of pace and can be measured more frequently than only every kilometer using my chronometer.

Note: of course with modern GPS-chronometer devices all metrics related with running speed can be monitored during the race directly by the runner at any given point. Personally I don´t want to measure my KPI´s with a higher frequency than once every kilometer, with the exception of the relative speed check during the end of the race. I also find a better harmony and stability in my running if I monitor and adjust only every five minutes which is roughly the time it takes me to run a kilometer during a marathon

CHAPTER 11
PASSION

"Without passion life is nothing"

Passion is a bit like Attitude. You can run a marathon and you can run a business without passion but just not as well as with passion. To be truly great at something in life you need to have true passion for it, may it be running a marathon, running a business, raising your children or just about anything in fact.

I found passion in running many years ago. I think what attracts me with running is the combination of physical effort, pushing your own limits, the feeling of progress during training and of course setting up and meeting a specific race objective. The additional kicks from racing down the beach with a bright full moon over the Mediterranean sea or those incredible runner´s high that give you intense shots of endorphin in your blood that makes you feel invincible and happy for some long pleasant seconds. When I went to ESADE business school some ago I realized the many parallels between the world of business and practicing sport. The marathon distance provided the perfect challenge and frame work to try out and develop the concept this book is based on. It took a couple of years to develop the concept. In 2012 I fully implemented it at the Barcelona marathon and managed to break my personal record by a full 20 minutes. I enjoyed every minute of the four months of preparation. It provided a great boost for self-confidence and it consolidated my passion for running.

In business I have found passion in different ways but what they all have in common is that my contribution has provided value to the stakeholders involved; colleagues, clients and partners. In my early career I ran a project to adapt a product range to the North American market, to later get the full product marketing responsibility during an expatriate mission in USA. Later on I introduced Spanish engineering services in technologically demanding markets such as Sweden, Germany, France and China. As responsible for the global business of the premium brand of an industrial assembly tool manufacturer, I had the opportunity to develop teams and businesses all over the world.

My professional life has also been marked by travel and languages. I find great passion in travelling and thereby meeting new people, learning about cultures, seeing different ways of life and learning how to do local business. Learning and interacting in different languages became a passion already during my university years and ever since do I use at least two different languages on a daily basis. Language is passion that I now pass onto my children who are trilingual and already starting to learn a fourth language.

CHAPTER 12
HAVE FUN

";-)"

Share blogs and create a social media group. Arrange mid-training BBQ with your running friends to run and eat together. This is what we did in 2012 when we prepared the Barcelona marathon and got together on a Saturday to run 20km along the beach, two of our kids even joined us on bikes, and continued with a fondue running party in the glazing Mediterranean February sun. On a personal level I created my own nickname for my first marathon: Gunnar The Runner.

Work can be fun. Creating great things is fun. Working in teams is fun. Seeing results from hard work is fun. At one company where we were around 10 different nationalities we would arrange a monthly Country Month lunch. So after the monthly meeting where I would present the results and upcoming activities, we would all join afterward for lunch prepared by one of the team members with flavors from his or her country of origin.

Fondue running party

CHAPTER 13
CHANGE MANAGEMENT*

"Be the change you want to see in the world."

In previous chapters we have gone through several values and compared their application on marathon running and running a business. So far the approach has been very generic regarding the business aspect, although relevant, in the different areas described.

Let´s see how the same concept can be applied to a more specific area; Change Management.

Step 1 - Create a sense of urgency

Step 2 - Form a guiding coalition

Step 3 - Develop a vision and strategy

Step 4 - Communicate the vision

Step 5 - Enabling action and removal of obstacles

Step 6 - Generating short-term wins

Step 7 - Don´t declare victory too soon

Step 8 - Anchor changes in the culture

*with pride inspired by Kotter´s 8-step change model

Gunnar Thorsén

CHAPTER 14
STEP 1 - CREATE A SENSE OF URGENCY

The reasons to run a marathon will be very different between individual runners; all from getting in shape for the beach season to pushing your limits by reaching an ambitious goal. I have found that the inertia needed from this step, in a marathon project is better achieved by generating an initial buzz together with other runners and then quickly build on that buzz with the following steps and some organized activities.

In a business environment creating a sense of urgency is the vital first step in order to get key stakeholders' attention and acceptance of the need for change. All subsequent steps will fail unless this first crucial step is performed successfully and with conviction. You need to be very clear about the situation and what has lead up to the need for change. It is better to be dramatic than mellow. If there ever is a time to cry wolf, this is it.

It is a common human reaction to want to resist change, or perhaps above all an initial resistance to be part of the change. Explain to the team what will be the consequences of not changing; as important as explaining the expected (positive) outcome of change.

To transmit the message it is essential to be physically present with the audience. An email or letter will not suffice. Of course the circumstances will depend on the size and geographical dispersion of the organization.

You may need to start with a smaller audience and have the message cascaded but the ideal scenario is to have everybody gathered in one place. Fly people in to join the meeting and make sure the entire leadership team is present.

There are two fundamental emotions you want to generate in people in order to create the sense of urgency and to get buy-in for the change project; fear and hope. Make sure you create these emotions in the right order; otherwise the effect will be the opposite. The most primordial human instinct is survival. Start by creating a sense of fear that will trigger an adrenaline rush and provoke a fight or flight reaction. Now the team is ready to take action. To avoid action turning into chaos and panic you need to continue to present the vision of the outcome of change and how it will be achieved; this will produce the sense of hope and confidence in the future.

CHAPTER 15
STEP 2 - FORM A GUIDING COALITION

Make sure your family supports the time and efforts you will invest during the months prior to race day. Form a small team of 2-6 people with the common goal of preparing and running the marathon. Your team will support, push, challenge and advice you during the preparation phase. Here is where the change leader will identify and define him-/herself.

Assure the support from key stakeholders in the initial phase of the change process. Characteristic for these stakeholders is that they have the power, formal or informal, to destroy the change process. The support by these stakeholders needs to be visible to the entire organization. You also need to create the team needed to implement the change process. It is often advisable to bring in external resources to be part of the change team. This will add credibility to the project and it will also bring in new ideas and competences.

Gunnar Thorsén

CHAPTER 16
STEP 3 - DEVELOP A VISION AND STRATEGY

Unless you have the capacity to finish in less than 2 hours and 15 minutes, forget about actually winning the marathon overall classification, regardless of gender and race location. Most likely you would need a finishing time close to 2 hours to actually have a chance to win the race. Thus, your vision and strategy should be personal. Be ambitious and realistic at the same time.

Example for a marathon project:

Vision: Learn from my marathon preparation to become a better family father and a more capable professional.

Strategy: My personal goal is to finish my first marathon and I aim to do it in less than 4 hours. To achieve this I will dedicate 3 days of training during 4 months.

Example for a business project:

Vision: To help our clients achieve their professional and personal ambitions through their language course abroad experience.

Strategy: Providing the largest selection of guaranteed high quality languages schools and creating the most user friendly and efficient online booking platform to find, select, enroll and pay for your language course.

In a business change management project all stakeholders must clearly see the reason for the change and why it is important. By explaining the strategy you will also assure that stakeholders support the project during the implementation.

CHAPTER 17
STEP 4 - COMMUNICATE THE VISION

Tell all your colleagues, friends and family that you will run the marathon. They will surely support you during the preparation but it also puts psychological pressure on you to follow through on your commitment. Personally I use blogs and social media to communicate with friends and family with updates and anecdotes from the change journey.

In the business change project it is especially important to communicate extensively the vision to all stakeholders throughout the project and to continuously maintain them updated during the implementation. The regular presence and hands-on attitude of the leadership team is very important to maintain momentum and motivation among the team members.

The first step to create a sense of urgency is best achieved in person and verbally. For the continuous communication other formats are suitable to assure the vision and strategy will be absorbed.

CHAPTER 18
STEP 5 – ENABLING ACTION AND REMOVAL OF OBSTACLES

Plan your training schedule for the entire preparation phase with day-by-day details on training type, intensity and duration. Make sure this training schedule is compatible with your work and family commitments. If weekly Sunday dinners at your mother-in-law's house collide with your weekly long distance run you need to make changes.

Running is a cheap activity. The only thing you must have to run a marathon is a good set of running shoes based on your running style and physical conditions. Visit a specialist store for advice on shoe models.

In business money and human resources are often scarce. Assure you have the budget and resources available to implement the change process. It is enough with one key stakeholder with the wrong attitude to run the change project into the grave. Either assure the support and commitment from this person or remove him/her from a position that can affect the project.

CHAPTER 19
STEP 6 – GENERATING SHORT-TERM WINS

Run intermediate shorter races such as 10 km and half marathons. This will boost your spirit as you see your improvements and will also give you confirmation if you are on right track to reach your goal.

Identify low hanging fruit in the early stages of the project and make them part of the strategy and project planning. The quick wins will boost morale and secure future support for the project by creating a positive atmosphere that will add to the feeling of hope that the vision of change will be bring a better future. Make sure you communicate these early wins throughout the organization and give deserving team members public credit for the accomplishments.

Gunnar Thorsén

CHAPTER 20
STEP 7 – DON´T DECLARE VICTORY TOO SOON

Running a half marathon at, for example, 1h 45m does not automatically mean that you will run the marathon at 3h 30m, in case this is your target finishing time. As a key performance indicator during your preparation period it would indicate that you are on the right track but don´t pop open the champagne just yet.

Also wait until after the race to make plans for your next race – stay focused!

The change project is not over until the change is firmly embedded in the corporate culture (see stage 8) and this is not done overnight. A successful change project will generate several short-term wins and at some point the initial fear and survival mode may disappear. This is dangerous to a change project. Make sure to remind the team that danger can return and that the project is not terminated just yet. Complacency is your biggest enemy at this point of the journey. Also beware of possible departures from the company of key stakeholders that have been firm supporters as this may reverse the changes.

CHAPTER 21
STEP 8 – ANCHOR CHANGES IN THE CULTURE

Use the momentum and adrenaline rush of the race day to get together with your team mates to celebrate having achieved your goals and start making plans for the next challenge. Make sure you always have another challenge to look forward to and plan for, always.

It will take time and more than one generation of management before the change can really be considered a part of corporate culture. A change project is different from the traditional definition of a project as it does not have a clearly defined end.

CHAPTER 22
IT WORKS!

In 2012 I managed to reach the most ambitious of my three race objectives, YEAH!, by following the advice outlined in this book and I finished at 3 hours 29 minutes 24 seconds, a full 20 minutes improvement over my previous personal best race time.

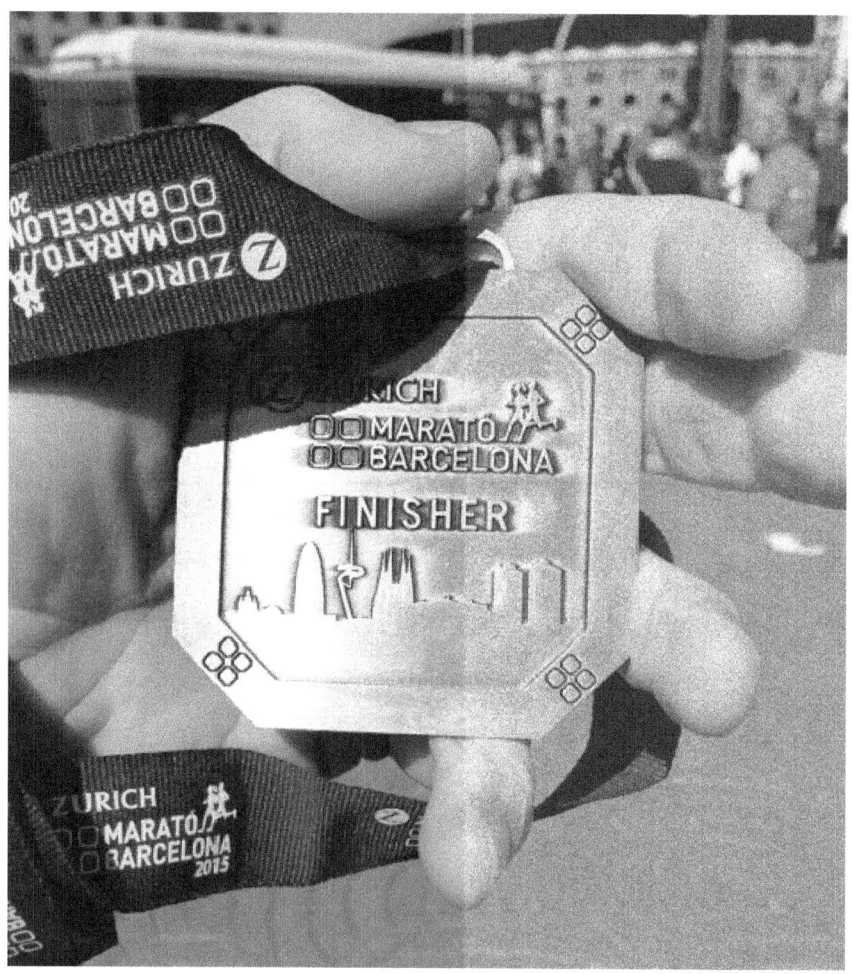

Marathon finisher medal 2015

QUICK GUIDES

Run Your Business like You run a Marathon

Running a Marathon	Running a Business
Attitude	
Anyone that wants to run a marathon can do so.	Anyone that wants to run a business can do so.
Ambition	
Push your limits beyond what you think you could do. In a marathon there are three basic goals. 1-train and show up on race day. 2-finish the race. 3-beat your personal record.	Why is your business only local when it can be nationwide? Why is your business only nationwide when it can be global? Think big!

Courage

You may fail. You may get injured. You may fail. You may not reach your objectives. You will suffer. Still you go for it knowing that to be a winner must take the leap. Be brave!

We mostly hear of the great successes but reality shows that most start-ups fail. Be brave!

Organization

Successfully preparing and running a marathon is not a coincidence, it requires planning with clear objectives, tasks and assigned resources.

Establish your short, mid and long term business objectives and establish a detailed action plan with milestones and deadlines that you stick to.

Team spirit

Even if marathon running in itself is an individual activity the most successful runners will train and compete as part of a team. Get inspiration and advice from fellow runners and enjoy sharing your own experiences with others.

You can start a business on your own but you cannot turn it into a great success without the help from others. Create a strong Team, believe in your Team, and inspire your Team.

Discipline

Stick to the training schedule, also on that rainy Monday evening in January.

Don´t be tempted to deviate from your business plan with every "unique" opportunity that comes up.

Sacrifice

You will invest time and efforts into the preparation phase, not only on race day.

Success comes from a little inspiration and a lot of hard work.

Flexibility

Unforeseen events will always occur. A business trip you did not expect, illness, minor injury, family issues, etc. Prepare your backup plan.

Even the best business plan is still only a plan based on projections. Make sure you can adapt to changing internal and external factors.

Perseverance

Follow through on your 3, 4 or 5 month schedule and complete the full 42.195 meters on race day.

Business success does not come overnight, keep up the momentum throughout you planning horizon.

Passion

Passion can be found in physical effort, pushing your limits, the feeling of progress and meeting a specific race objective.

Passion in business can be adding customer value or develop as a professional. Find your passion!

Have FUN

Share blogs and create a social media group. Arrange mid-training BBQ with your running friends.

Work can be fun. Creating great things is fun. Working in teams is fun. Seeing results from hard work is fun.

Gunnar Thorsén

Change management*

Running a Marathon	Running a Change process
1. Create a sense of urgency	
Individual reasons to run a marathon will be very different; all from getting in shape for the beach season to pushing your limits by reaching an ambitious goal.	The vital first step in order to get key stakeholder's attention and acceptance of the need for change.
2. Form a guiding coalition	
Make sure your family supports you. Form a small team of 2-6 people with the common goal of the marathon. Your team will support, push, challenge and advice you during the preparation phase.	Assure the support from key stakeholders in the initial phase of the change process. You also need to create the team needed to implement the change process.
3. Develop a vision and strategy	
Your vision and strategy should be personal. Be ambitious and realistic at the same time.	In a business change management project all stakeholders must clearly see the reason for the change and why it is important.

4. Communicate the vision

Tell all your friends and family that you will run the marathon. They will support you and it also puts psychological pressure on you to follow through on your commitment.

Important to communicate extensively the vision to all stakeholders early in the project as well as continuously maintain them updated during the implementation.

5. Enabling action and removal of obstacle

Plan your training schedule for the entire preparation phase. Day by day with details on training intensity and duration. Make sure this training schedule is compatible with your work and family commitments.

Assure you have the budget and resources available to implement the change process. It is enough with one key stakeholder to run the change project into the grave. Either assure the support or remove this person from a position that can affect the project.

6. Generating short-term wins

Run intermediate shorter races such as 10 km and half marathons. This will boost your spirit as you see your improvements and will also give you confirmation if you are on right track to reach your goal.

Identify low hanging fruit in the early stages of the project to assure quick wins to boost morale and secure future support for the project. Also make sure you communicate these early wins throughout the organization.

7. Don´t declare victory too soon

Running a half marathon at 1h 45m does NOT automatically mean that you will run the marathon at 3h 30m. Also wait until after the race to make plans for your next race – stay focused!

The change project is not over until the change is firmly embedded in the corporate culture (see step 8) and this is not done overnight. Also the departure from the company of key stakeholders that have been firm supporters may reverse the changes.

8. Anchor changes in the culture

Use the momentum and adrenaline rush of the race day to get together with your team mates to celebrate having achieved your goals and start making plans for the next challenge.

This will take time and more than one generation of management before the change can really be considered a part of corporate culture. A change project is different from the traditional definition of a project as it does not have a clearly defined end.

*with pride inspired by Kotter´s 8-step change model

ABOUT THE AUTHOR

With many years as a successful business professional and with several marathons under his belt, Gunnar Thorsén shows the reader how to apply several key skill-sets in business practice to the preparation and running of a marathon race. Gunnar also puts his feet where his mouth is. As an example one marathon race objective was to reach a very ambitious personal objective that represented a 9% (20 minutes) improvement over the personal best mark achieved the previous year. This objective was reached by following the principles and ideas outlined in this book.

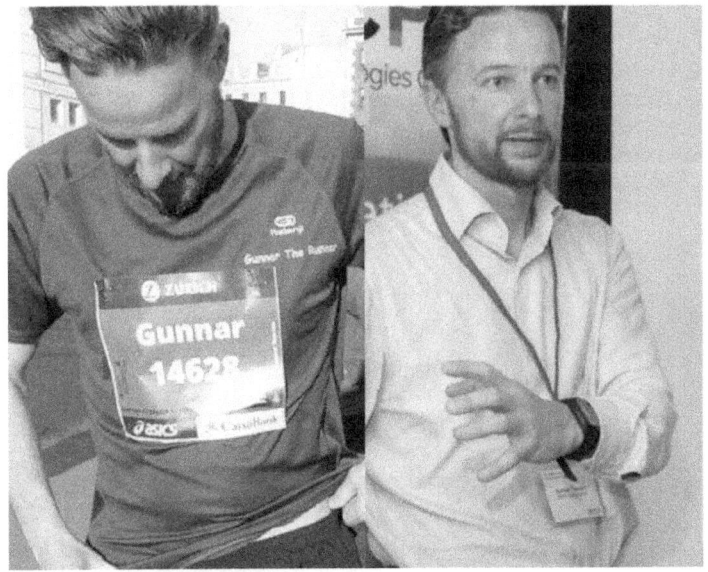

www.ingramcontent.com/pod-product-compliance
Lightning Source LLC
Chambersburg PA
CBHW061200180526
45170CB00002B/886